ZERO ANXIETY HOME-BUYING

ZERO ANXIETY HOME-BUYING

SIMPLIFIED-HOMEBUYING EXPERT

NILESH VOHRA

ANKITA OSWAL   NAVJOT SINGH BHAMRA

Worldwide Published by

Pendown Press

PENDOWN PRESS LLP

An ISO 9001 & ISO 14001 Certified Co.,

Regd. Office: 3767A, Kanhaiya Nagar,
Tri Nagar, Delhi-110035
Ph.: 8130886000, 9650072927
E-mail: info@pendownpress.com
Branch Office: 1A/2A, 20, Hari Sadan, Ansari Road,
Daryaganj, New Delhi-110002
Ph.: 011-45794768
Website: PendownPress.com

Edition: 2024
Price: ₹ 499
ISBN: 978-93-6338-739-3

Layout and Cover Designed by Pendown Graphics Team
Printed and Bound in India by Thomson Press India Ltd.

CONTENTS

PREFACE

Welcome to **"Zero Anxiety Home-Buying- 17 Must-Know Secrets Before Buying Your Dream "**

Buying a home is one of the most significant investments you'll ever make, and while it is, and should be an exhilarating experience, if both you and me were to be honest, it is often riddled with constant self-doubt & sleepless nights at its best and mind-numbing & physically debilitating anxiety at it's worst.

Whether you're a first-time homebuyer or looking to upgrade your current living situation, the journey to finding your dream home is filled with potential pitfalls and challenges.

As a second-generation realtor, I have seen this anxiety up close in my extended family, friends and clients. I see their hopes and dreams when buying or upgrading a home and I also see their dreams shattered. Imagine, your life's earnings go into buying a home, if you are amongst the majority, you will be buying a home today and paying a major chunk of your earnings as EMI for the next 20 years at the very least. It's not a decision that can be taken lightly!

So, why do their dreams get shattered? Simple, because they don't know how to choose the right home that is a good fit for them. They don't know because they have never been taught it and the world of real estate is not easy to navigate, it is not a straightforward world where what you see is what you get. It is a world where promises made are not always kept.

To find your dream home that will not turn into a nightmare once bought, you as a buyer need to do due diligence and to do this successfully, you must know what to look for by scratching the surface gloss and digging deep.

That is why I decided to use my years of learning and hands-on experience to guide home buyers and equip them with confidence to make the process joyful and meaningful instead of anxiety-ridden and so this book.

This book is designed to guide you through the complex process of home buying with insider knowledge and practical tips. Over the years, I've seen firsthand the common mistakes and misconceptions that can lead to costly errors.

The 17 secrets revealed in this book are based on my extensive experience and are aimed at empowering you to make informed decisions.

By understanding these secrets, you'll be better equipped to avoid the common traps that many homebuyers fall into. You'll learn how to identify your needs and priorities, understand market trends, negotiate effectively, and make sound financial decisions. Each chapter is dedicated to a specific aspect of the home-buying process, providing you with actionable advice and insights.

As you embark on this journey, remember that knowledge is power. The more informed you are, the more confident you'll be in making the right choices for you and your family.

This book will serve as a valuable resource, helping you achieve your goal of finding the perfect home without unnecessary stress or regret.

Thank you for choosing to read this book. I am excited to share these secrets with you and look forward to guiding you toward a successful and rewarding home-buying experience.

Happy home hunting!

Nilesh Vohra

Navigating The Home-Buying Maze: Setting Context

Buying a home(s) is one of the most significant decisions you will ever make. It often involves investing your life's savings into a single purchase, which makes it crucial to approach this journey with care, knowledge, and thorough preparation.

As a conscious and ethical real estate entrepreneur, I understand the weight of this decision and value the trust you place in your builder. It is this sense of responsibility to live up to the expectations and trust of the buyers that lies at the core of my business and the intent behind writing this book.

This book,

"Zero Anxiety Home-Buying- 17 Must-Know Secrets Before Buying Your Dream " is designed to equip you—the homebuyer with the essential insights and secrets that often remain untold, but are vital for making an informed choice. And believe me, as a 2nd generation real estate entrepreneur having a hands-on experience of 15+ years, I do know this biz inside out and have quite a bit of tea to spill.

The Importance of Due Diligence

Like in most other areas, in the world of real estate too, knowledge is power. The journey to owning a home is filled with excitement, anticipation, and sometimes, anxiety. You are not just buying a piece of property; you are investing in a future, a lifestyle, and a sanctuary for you and your family.

This book aims to provide you with a reality check & practical tools that will help you navigate this complex process with confidence and minimal anxiety. By understanding the secrets and conducting thorough due diligence, you can safeguard your hard-earned money and ensure that your investment is sound.

Decoding The Buyer-Builder Relationship: The 4 Touch Points

The relationship between a home buyer and a builder can be defined through four major touch points, each playing a crucial role in shaping the overall experience of the buyer:

1. **Pre-Sales and Sales:** This is the initial phase where the builder obviously puts their best foot forward. You are wooed with promises, polished presentations, and a showcase of their best work. This phase is generally all song & dance and cheese & wine— It's designed to be an overwhelmingly positive experience aimed at securing your commitment.
2. **CRM/Post-Sales:** Once you've succumbed to the serenade and signed on the dotted line, the focus shifts. After the purchase of an under-construction property, the focus automatically shifts to the construction phase. The builder is expected to complete the project on time and maintain the promised quality, while you, the buyer, are expected to make timely payments. This phase also includes any customization requests, their responses and the resultant experiences you may have.
3. **Handover:** This critical stage involves delivering the apartment and meeting the quality and timeline expectations set earlier. It also includes the transition of society and maintenance

responsibilities to the residents' association, a big milestone and shift indeed!

4. **Post-Handover and Loyalty:** As a client, ensuring that there are no issues once you move in and the resolution of any that arise promptly is essential for maintaining a positive experience. The goal for the builder is to elevate your satisfaction and build lasting trust.

While the pre-sales phase is often filled with care and exceptional service, it is during the later stages that the true nature of the builder becomes apparent, however, by then it is too late. You are already in too deep—

In the Pre-sales stage, is it possible to judge what experiences you may have in the following 3 stages? It is certainly possible to get a basic sense at the very least of what might be in store for you. This book will guide you through each phase, helping you to identify red flags before committing and once committed, making informed decisions that protect your investment.

Is Your Builder Showing You Their Authentic Face, Or Wearing A Mask?

Without prejudice and with immense respect for all the authentic entities of the community, it wouldn't be wrong to say that builders often put up a great face during the pre-sales and sales phases, going the extra mile to seduce buyers with impeccable service and attractive offers. However, the true measure of a builder's reliability and ethics becomes evident in the later stages—post-sales, handover, and post-handover. This book is intended as your guide to seeing beyond the polished façade and understanding the real dynamics at play.

By sharing these 17 secrets, I hope to empower you with the knowledge to conduct thorough due diligence, ask the right questions, and make informed decisions. From reading a RERA page and checking the legacy of the developer to understanding the customization flexibility and knowing your rights as a home buyer, this book covers all the essential aspects that you need to consider.

Hitting Bulls Eye

Your home is more than just a place to live; it is a reflection of your dreams, aspirations, and hard work. Making the right choice involves more than just liking the design or the location. It requires a deep understanding of the builder's credibility, the quality of construction, the transparency of dealings, and the level of post-purchase support you can expect.

As you embark on this journey, let this book be your trusted companion. Armed with these 17 secrets, you will be better equipped to navigate the complexities of home-buying, avoid common pitfalls, and make a decision that you will cherish for years to come. Your home-buying experience should be positive and fulfilling, and with the right knowledge, it can be.

Welcome to the "17 Secrets Every Home Buyer Needs to Know." Let's begin this journey together, ensuring that your path to homeownership is as smooth, secure, and rewarding as possible.

SECRET 1

Leveraging RERA
Your Home Buying Shield

Buying a home is one of the most significant decisions you will ever make. It involves a substantial financial commitment and emotional investment.

As you navigate this journey, it's crucial to leverage every tool at your disposal to ensure a safe and informed purchase. One such tool, particularly potent in India, is the Real Estate (Regulation and Development) Act, 2016 (RERA).

Understanding and leveraging RERA intelligence can be your shield against potential pitfalls in the home-buying process. Let's delve into the art of leveraging RERA, with real-life stories to illustrate its importance.

The Power of RERA

The Real Estate (Regulation and Development) Act, 2016, commonly known as RERA was introduced to bring transparency, accountability, and efficiency to the real estate sector. It aims to protect home buyers and ensure that builders deliver on their promises.

Here's how you can leverage RERA to your advantage:

Key Benefits of RERA for Homebuyers

1. **Accountability**: Developers are now held accountable for their promises. Buyers can seek redressal for any deviations or fraudulent activities.
2. **Transparency**: Information regarding the financial health of the project, including how funds are being used, is available to the buyers.
3. **Legal Recourse**: RERA provides a platform for buyers to file complaints and seek redressal. The completion date mentioned on the RERA registration is legally binding, and buyers are entitled to compensation if the developer fails to meet this deadline.
4. **State-Specific Authorities**: RERA has been implemented across 22 states and 6 union territories, each with its own RERA authority and website.

How To Leverage RERA

1. **Research and Verify Project Registration:** Always start by checking the RERA registration status of the project and the builder. Use the official RERA website for your state to verify all details.

   Before committing to a property, ensure that the project is registered under RERA. This registration ensures that the builder adheres to the regulations and provides a level of transparency about the project.

   Priya and Rajesh, a young couple in Pune, were looking at a new housing project and were on the verge of committing. Urged by a friend, they visited the RERA website and discovered that the project was not listed. Digging deeper, they found that the builder had a history of delays and legal issues. Thanks to RERA, they avoided a potentially troublesome investment.

2. **Check Project Details:** RERA mandates that all registered projects disclose crucial information, including project plans, approvals, and timelines. This transparency allows you to verify the authenticity and status of the project.

   Kavita, a marketing professional in Mumbai, was interested in an upcoming project. By checking the RERA website, she found detailed information about the project's progress, legal approvals, and expected completion date. This transparency gave her confidence in the builder's commitment and she ended up buying a home in that project, a decision that she believes bettered her life

3. **Check Developer's Background:** Do a thorough background check on the developer's legacy and reputation. Look into any past projects and customer reviews.

   Check Project Timeline: Compare the RERA-stated completion date with any verbal commitments made by the developer. A buffer of 12 to 18 months is reasonable, but anything beyond that should raise concerns. Inspect the project site physically to assess the progress and compare it with the timeline and milestones mentioned on RERA.

4. **Check Financial Health:** Assess if there are any legal or financial encumbrances on the project. This includes checking for any ongoing litigations or mortgages on the project land.

   Additionally, there are two more benefits that you can leverage and will come in useful in all the stages of the home-buying to home-possession process.

5. **Understand Your Rights:** RERA provides specific rights to home buyers, including timely possession, quality construction, and the right to withdraw from a project if there are significant delays or discrepancies.

   Amit and Sneha, a couple from Delhi, faced significant delays in the handover of their apartment. They leveraged RERA's provisions to file a complaint and were compensated for the delay. Their awareness of their rights under RERA saved them from financial strain and ensured they were treated fairly.

6. **Access to Legal Recourse:** If a builder fails to deliver as promised, RERA provides a platform for grievance redressal. Home buyers can file complaints and seek resolution through the RERA authority. Suresh, a software engineer from Bangalore, found major construction defects in his new apartment. He filed a complaint with the RERA authority and received a prompt resolution, ensuring the defects were rectified at the builder's expense.

Leveraging RERA is essential for making a safe and informed home-buying decision. By ensuring that a project is registered and understanding the details and your rights, you can protect your investment and avoid common pitfalls. Priya and Rajesh, Kavita, Amit and Sneha, and Suresh all benefited from using RERA as their shield. With the right knowledge and approach, you too can navigate the complexities of home buying with confidence.

Remember, RERA is more than just a regulatory requirement; it's a powerful tool designed to protect you. Use it wisely, and let it guide you towards a secure and satisfying home-buying experience.

SECRET 2

Know Your Developer:
Dig Deep Before You Decide

Know Your Developer - Dig Deep Before You Decide

Investing in a home is one of the most significant financial decisions you'll ever make. Yet, many buyers don't thoroughly investigate the developer of their future home. Knowing your developer inside and out can save you from future headaches and financial losses. Here's how you can make sure you're choosing the right developer for your dream home.

The Importance of Knowing Your Developer

When you buy a home, you are not just buying a piece of property; you are also investing in the developer's reputation, reliability, and track record. A credible developer can ensure timely delivery, quality construction, and adherence to promises made. On the other hand, a developer with a shaky past can turn your dream into a nightmare.

Steps to Vet Your Developer

1. **Research the Developer's Background:**
    - **Past Projects:** Look into the developer's completed projects. For instance, if you're considering a project

by ABC Builders, check how their previous projects like ABC Heights or ABC Residency have fared. Were they completed on time? Are the residents satisfied?

- **Online Reviews:** Platforms like Google Reviews, mouthshut.com, social media, and real estate forums can provide valuable insights. Take the example of Mr. Sanjay, who found numerous complaints about delayed possession and poor construction quality for a project he was interested in. He wisely decided to look for a more reliable developer.

2. **Financial Stability:**
   - **Company's Financial Health:** A financially stable developer is more likely to complete the project on time. Check their financial reports if available, or seek advice from financial experts.
   - **Funding Sources:** Ensure the project is not overly dependent on pre-sales and has secured funding from reputed financial institutions.
3. **Legal Compliance and Transparency:**
   - **RERA Registration:** Verify that the project is registered with RERA and that all details are transparent. The RERA page should provide comprehensive information about the project, including timelines, approvals, and litigations.
   - **Legal Clearances:** Ensure the project has all necessary approvals and clearances. Rajeev a businessman, once nearly invested in a project that lacked environmental clearance, which would have caused legal issues down the line.

4. Assessing the Developer's Legal Standing:

When purchasing a home, understanding the legal standing of your developer is crucial. A developer embroiled in numerous legal battles can indicate potential risks and complications. Here are the key points to consider when evaluating the legal aspects of your developer:

- **Litigious Personality:** Research whether the developer has a history of being litigious. This can be an indicator of how they handle disputes and conflicts, which might eventually affect you as a buyer.
- **Ongoing Legal Cases:** Investigate how many legal cases the developer is currently involved in. A high number of ongoing cases, whether civil or criminal, can be a red flag about the developer's operational integrity and business practices.
- **Size Of The Legal Department:** Assess the size of the developer's legal department. A large legal team might indicate frequent legal issues, while a smaller team might suggest fewer legal complications. However, it can also reflect the scale of the developer's operations, so consider the situation in context.
- **Customer Litigations:** Determine how many litigations the developer has faced from customers. Frequent customer disputes can signal dissatisfaction with the developer's services, quality, or adherence to commitments.
- **Disputes with Completed Societies and Resident Associations:** Check for any legal battles with societies or resident associations. Such litigations often arise from

unresolved issues post-completion, such as maintenance, amenities, or structural defects.

- **Litigations with Investors and Financial Institutions:** Look into any ongoing or past litigations with investors, financiers, or banks. These disputes can indicate financial instability or mismanagement.

Why It Matters

Understanding these aspects helps you gauge the reliability and trustworthiness of the developer. A developer with a clean legal record is likely to be more trustworthy and reliable, ensuring a smoother home-buying experience. In contrast, a developer with numerous legal issues might pose risks and lead to complications during and after the purchase.

Key Indicators of a Reputable Developer

1. **Quality of Construction:** Visit previous projects to assess the construction quality. Speak to current residents about their experiences.
2. **Timely Delivery:** A developer with a history of delivering projects on or before the promised date is a positive sign. Mr. Arun chose XYZ Developers because their past projects were consistently delivered ahead of schedule.
3. **Post-Sales Service:** Reliable developers offer excellent post-sales service, addressing issues promptly even after possession.

The Escalation Matrix

Understanding the escalation matrix of the builder is crucial for addressing issues effectively. A good developer will have a clear and transparent process for handling grievances. This should include:

1. **Customer Support:** Initial point of contact for any issues. Ensure the support team is responsive and helpful.
2. **Project Manager:** If the issue isn't resolved by customer support, it should be escalated to the project manager.
3. **Senior Management:** Persistent issues should be directed to the senior management team. Reputable developers will ensure that concerns reaching this level are addressed swiftly and satisfactorily.

By thoroughly vetting your developer, you can make an informed decision and avoid potential pitfalls. Remember, a little due diligence now can save you from significant troubles later. So, dig deep, ask questions, and ensure you are putting your hard-earned money into the right hands.

❍ ❍ ❍ ❍

SECRET 3

Customization Flexibility
Tailoring Your Dream Home

Buying a home is a deeply personal experience. It's not just about finding a place to live; it's about creating a space that reflects your personality, meets your needs, and fits your lifestyle. One of the key aspects to consider when purchasing a new home is customization flexibility. This secret will unveil how you can leverage customization options to make your dream home truly your own, while also sharing tips and real-life examples to guide you through the process.

Understanding Customization Flexibility

Customization flexibility refers to the ability to alter or upgrade various elements of your home to better suit your preferences. This can range from minor modifications like choosing the color of your walls or the type of flooring, to more significant changes like altering the layout or adding additional rooms. **Understanding the extent of customization offered by the developer is crucial before finalizing your purchase.**

Why Customization Matters

Imagine you've found the perfect location, the ideal neighborhood, and a house with great potential. However, the kitchen is too small, the master bedroom lacks a walk-in closet, and the living room doesn't have enough natural light.

Wouldn't you be disappointed?

Customization flexibility allows you to address these issues, ensuring your new home matches your vision.

The Customization Journey: A Real-Life Example

Consider the story of Rahulj and Shriya, a young couple from Bangalore. They were excited to buy their first home but had specific requirements. Rahul loves to cook, so a spacious, well-designed kitchen was a must. Shriya works from home and needs a dedicated office space. The standard layout of the homes they were looking at didn't quite meet these needs.

However, they chose a developer known for offering extensive customization options. The developer allowed them to extend the kitchen, incorporate a home office, and even add a skylight in the living room to enhance natural light. **Rahul and Shriya's dream home became a reality, thanks to the flexibility provided by their developer.**

Tips for Leveraging Customization Options

1. **Research Your Developer:** Not all developers offer the same level of customization. Investigate the extent of modifications allowed and check reviews or testimonials from previous buyers.
2. **Ask for a Customization Guide:** Many developers provide a customization guide detailing what changes can be made, associated costs, and timelines. This document can be invaluable in planning your modifications.

3. **Plan Your Changes Early:** The earlier you decide on customizations, the better. Early planning helps avoid delays and additional costs.
4. **Prioritize Your Needs:** Determine what changes are non-negotiable and what can be compromised. This will help in managing your budget and expectations.
5. **Get Everything in Writing:** Ensure all agreed-upon customizations are documented in your contract to avoid disputes later.

Realistic Expectations and Potential Pitfalls

While customization offers many benefits, it's important to have realistic expectations. Some developers may have limitations on what can be altered due to structural or regulatory reasons. Additionally, extensive customization can increase the overall cost and extend the construction timeline.

Sunil and Antara, a couple from Pune, had a different experience. They were initially thrilled with the customization options offered by their developer. However, midway through the construction, they faced issues with the quality of materials used and delays in completion. This situation underscores the importance of choosing a reputable developer and ensuring thorough communication and documentation of all customization agreements.

Making Your Home Truly Yours

Customization flexibility is a powerful tool in transforming a house into your dream home. By understanding your options, planning carefully, and choosing a trustworthy developer, you can tailor your new home to perfectly fit your needs and desires. Remember, your home is a reflection of you, and with the right approach, you can make it truly yours.

Embrace the opportunity to customize, but stay informed and vigilant to ensure a smooth and satisfying home-buying experience. Your dream home is not just a place to live; it's a space that embodies your unique lifestyle and aspirations.

SECRET 4

Beyond The Gloss
Know The Real Minds Behind the Project

When investing in a home, it's crucial to look beyond the glossy brochures and attractive models. Understanding the people behind the project—the developer, the architects, the engineers, and the project managers—can give you invaluable insights into the reliability and quality of your future home.

This secret focuses on how to uncover the real minds behind the project and why this knowledge is essential for making an informed decision.

The Importance of Knowing the Team

The success of a real estate project largely depends on the competence and integrity of the team responsible for its execution. **A project might look great on paper, but the actual delivery depends on the skills, experience, and reputation of the people involved.**

a. **Architect**

   Vision of the Architect:

   - The architect's vision is crucial as it sets the tone for the entire project. Understanding their USPs (Unique Selling Propositions) will give you insight into the innovative aspects they bring to the project.

Orientation and Arrangement of Buildings:

- Examine how the buildings are oriented and arranged. Proper orientation can enhance privacy, natural light, and ventilation. For instance, are the buildings designed to ensure that one cannot easily see into other apartments? This aspect of design is essential for maintaining privacy.

Privacy:

- Investigate how private the apartments are. What portion of the house is visible to visitors from the entrance? The design should ideally separate public spaces (like living rooms) from private ones (like bedrooms).

Building Distance and Layout:

- Check the distance between houses on the same floor. Adequate spacing prevents overcrowding and ensures a comfortable living environment. Are there foyers at the entrance to add an extra layer of privacy and separation of public and private spaces?

Outside Elevation:

- The outside elevation is another critical aspect. Will you see ducts, AC units, kitchens, and dry balconies from outside when you enter the premises? A well-thought-out design hides these elements, maintaining a clean and attractive facade.

b. Landscape Architect

Vision of the Landscape Architect:

- The landscape architect's vision is crucial in creating a harmonious and aesthetically pleasing environment. It's essential to understand the end-use studies they conducted and why they selected the specific amenities. For instance, did they focus on creating a green oasis with ample walking paths, or did they prioritize recreational facilities for families?

Expertise in Trees and Plants:

- Verify if the landscape architect is an expert on trees and plants. A knowledgeable landscape architect will select flora that is not only visually appealing but also suitable for the local climate and soil, ensuring long-term sustainability and low maintenance.
- What is the overarching vision for the plantations? Is it to create a lush, green environment, to enhance biodiversity, or to provide shaded areas for relaxation? Understanding this vision will help you appreciate the thought and planning that went into the landscaping.

Naina & Vineet were looking for a project with extensive green spaces and recreational facilities. They chose a development where the landscape architect had a clear vision of creating a green oasis with native plants, ensuring both beauty and sustainability.

Gym Design

Fitness Expertise:

➢ The design of the gym is another critical aspect. It's important to know who is designing the gym and whether the landscape architect has a fitness consultant on board. A well-designed gym by a fitness expert will ensure that the equipment layout is optimal for various workouts and that the space is safe and user-friendly.

Sunil, an avid fitness enthusiast, chose a project where the gym was designed by a renowned fitness expert. The expert's involvement ensured that the gym was equipped with state-of-the-art equipment and had a layout that facilitated effective workouts.

Mini-Theatre Design

Sound Expertise:

- The mini-theatre is a valuable amenity for many residents if you are one of them. Ensure that the person designing the mini-theatre understands sound design. This expertise is crucial for creating an immersive audio-visual experience.

c. **Structural Design Consultant**

First off, you need to check whether the project is a high-rise or a low-rise structure. If the project is a high-rise building then check to ensure that all the rules and regulations for highrise constructions have been followed. Also check does the structural consultant has the requisite expertise and experience in constructing high-rise buildings. Ensure they have a solid track record of successfully completed high-rise structures.

d. **MEP (Mechanical, Electrical, Plumbing) Consultant**

When choosing your dream home, ensure that you delve into the expertise, experience and reputation & credibility of the MEP (Mechanical, Electrical, and Plumbing) consultants. This is the consultant whose work is going to have the most impact on your day-to-day living efficiency and convenience.

Consider their experience and expertise in projects of similar scale and complexity. Check their qualifications, certifications, and professional affiliations to ensure they meet industry standards. Understand whether the MEP consultant for the project has done end-use studies to understand what you, the end user need.

Even simple things such as the number & placement of charging points, or where to have two-way switches can make or ruin your daily living experience. Thus you can imagine how the right/wrong MEP Consultant could impact your choice. Evaluate their understanding of regulations, and sustainable design practices. Review their portfolio to see previous work and innovations in energy efficiency, HVAC systems, electrical distribution, and plumbing solutions.

e. Fire Safety Consultant

When buying a property, considering fire safety is crucial for ensuring the safety of occupants and compliance with legal requirements. Find out if the property has a dedicated fire safety consultant or not. If not then it's a definite no go, if yes then here are some key points to keep in mind regarding fire safety consultants when buying a property:

- Ensure the fire safety consultant is qualified, certified, and has a good track record.
- Check their portfolio and see if they have relevant experience working on properties similar to the one you are purchasing.
- The consultant should be knowledgeable about local fire safety regulations and building codes.
- They should ensure that the property complies with all current fire safety standards and should have conducted a thorough fire safety assessment of the property.

- This assessment should include checking fire exits, fire alarms, sprinklers, and fire-resistant materials. The consultant should identify potential fire hazards and provide recommendations to mitigate them. They should evaluate the overall fire risk and suggest improvements or upgrades if necessary.
- Ensure the property has adequate fire safety systems in place, such as smoke detectors, fire alarms, and sprinkler systems.
- The consultant should verify that all fire safety equipment is functioning correctly and is regularly maintained.
- Check for Fire Escape Evacuation Plans and Emergency Procedures. Is there a clear fire escape plan and route? Is there a clear path for the fire tender to reach the affected areas in every area of the building? Are the fire safety arrangements commensurate with the population of the building? Will it be easy and quick to reach the refuge areas in case of a fire emergency?
- Will the consultants provide training for occupants on fire safety awareness and emergency response ensuring that all occupants know the evacuation routes and emergency protocols.?
- Will there be regular fire drills and safety training sessions conducted for staff & residents of the building?
- Checking for all these points will help you make a safe and informed decision regarding your dream home.

f. Traffic Consultant

When searching for your dream home, it's essential to consider whether the project has a traffic consultant involved. In today's densely populated societies, managing traffic flow is crucial, especially during peak hours in the morning when driveways and one-way streets can become highly congested. Effective traffic management can significantly reduce inconvenience, and delays, and ensure a smoother daily routine.

Here's why it's essential to choose a project that has a traffic consultant on board-

- A traffic consultant is a professional who specializes in planning and managing traffic flow within residential areas. Their expertise ensures that traffic is organized efficiently, minimizing congestion and delays.
- During peak hours, especially in the mornings, traffic can become a significant issue in densely populated societies. A traffic consultant can design and implement strategies to manage these busy periods effectively. Proper route planning within the society can prevent bottlenecks and ensure the smooth movement of vehicles. This includes planning for entry and exit points, parking areas, and internal roadways.
- A traffic consultant can also enhance the safety of residents by designing pedestrian-friendly pathways, ensuring proper signage, and implementing speed control measures.
- A traffic consultant can design traffic pathways to maximize space and minimize conflicts between moving vehicles and parked cars.
- A traffic consultant on board would also ensure that emergency vehicles have unobstructed access. A traffic consultant can plan routes that facilitate quick and easy

access for fire trucks, ambulances, and other emergency services.

Long-term Benefits:

- Effective traffic management not only provides immediate benefits by enhancing the overall living experience but can be a significant factor in the property's appreciation over time.
- By ensuring that your potential new home has a traffic consultant involved in its planning and development, you can enjoy a more convenient, efficient, and safer living environment. This foresight will not only improve your daily commute but also enhance the overall quality of life within the community.

g. Facade & Lighting Consultant

A facade and lighting consultant plays a crucial role in property projects by enhancing both the aesthetic appeal and functional aspects of buildings.

Not every project will have a facade & lighting consultant on board, however, the external appearance of the building to begin with and down the line is important. You wouldn't want to live in a dilapidated-looking building for sure or want to pay heavy maintenance on its upkeep frequently. So, if you find a property with a facade consultant on board that meets all your other criteria as well, go for it!

A facade consultant specializes in the design and engineering of the building's exterior, ensuring it meets aesthetic, functional, and structural requirements.

They select materials that enhance appearance, ensure structural integrity, and contribute to energy efficiency. Their role includes optimizing insulation, reducing thermal bridging, and integrating shading devices. They also focus on weatherproofing, durability, compliance with local building codes, and incorporating fire safety measures. Sustainability is another key aspect, promoting the use of eco-friendly materials and design features like green walls or solar panels.

On the lighting part, the consultant designs effective lighting systems for exterior spaces & public interiors as well, enhancing functionality and aesthetics while ensuring energy efficiency. They develop comprehensive lighting plans, recommend energy-efficient solutions such as LED lighting, and maximize natural light usage. Their designs consider factors like color temperature, glare control, and support for circadian rhythms to promote occupant health and well-being.

This secret will help you peek behind the scenes and truly understand whether the project truly has some brilliant, experienced and innovative minds backing it or is merely a touched-up gloss on paper.

SECRET 5

Beyond Face Value
Unmasking Hidden Costs

Buying a home is a significant investment, and it's crucial to understand the various charges that may be hidden in the fine print of your real estate contract. In Indian real estate, there are several fees and charges that home buyers need to be aware of to avoid any surprises down the line.

Here are some key points to consider when checking for hidden charges before making your purchase:

1. **Cancellation Charges:** It's essential to thoroughly understand the cancellation policy in your agreement. Some developers impose hefty charges if you decide to back out of the deal.
2. **Nomination/Name Change Charges:** If you plan to transfer the property to another party, there may be additional fees involved. Make sure these charges are transparent from the beginning.
3. **EDC (External Development Charges):** These charges are imposed by the government for developing infrastructure around the property. Ensure that you know how much you are liable to pay.
4. **Club Charges:** If your property comes with club membership or access to amenities, there might be separate charges

associated with it. Verify these costs beforehand, don't just assume that the club membership is a part of the package by default.

5. **Maintenance Deposit:** Some developers ask for an upfront maintenance deposit. Understand the purpose of this deposit and whether it's refundable.
6. **Interest Charges:** In case of delays in payments, developers might charge interest. Clarify the interest rate and conditions under which it will be applicable.
7. **GST (Goods and Services Tax):** Be aware of the GST implications on your property purchase. Understand how much GST you need to pay and factor this into your budget.
8. **PLC (Preferential Location Charges):** If you are opting for a specific location within a project, there could be extra charges associated with it. Confirm the PLC and its implications.
9. **FEC (Floor Escalation Charges):** Builders sometimes charge extra if you buy a flat on a higher floor. Know the FEC applicable in your case.

By familiarizing yourself with these hidden charges and ensuring clarity on each aspect, you can make a well-informed decision when buying a home in the Indian real estate market.

❍ ❍ ❍ ❍

SECRET 6

Navigating Customer Relationships
The Critical Role of CRM

When it comes to purchasing a home, the attitude and effectiveness of the Customer Relationship Management (CRM) team play a pivotal role in ensuring a smooth and satisfactory experience for the buyer. While the sales team may be welcoming and accommodating during the initial stages, customers need to assess the CRM team carefully before committing to a purchase.

Here are key points to consider when evaluating the CRM team:

- **Approachability and Expertise:** How accessible and experienced is the CRM team? Are they senior enough to handle and resolve your concerns effectively? It's crucial to have competent professionals who can address your queries and provide solutions promptly.
- **Maturity and Understanding:** Do members of the CRM team demonstrate maturity in handling customer issues? Are they empathetic and capable of understanding the significance of your concerns as a home buyer? Look for a team that can connect with your perspective and prioritize your needs.
- **Query Resolution in Agreements:** Before signing any agreements related to the sale, ensure that the CRM team

satisfactorily addresses all your queries and clarifications. Clear communication and transparency at this stage are key to avoiding future misunderstandings.

- **Home Loan Assistance Team:** Evaluate the ease of interaction with the home loan assistance team. They should be efficient, proactive, and supportive in guiding you through the financial aspects of your purchase.
- **Mindfulness and Customer-Centric Approach:** It is paramount for the CRM team to appreciate the gravity of the home-buying decision for the customer. Any employee who trivializes this significant life milestone is doing a disservice to both the customer and the developer. The CRM team must acknowledge that the customer is embarking on a long-term commitment and treat them as partners in the home-buying journey.

By scrutinizing the CRM team based on these criteria, you can ensure that they receive the support, understanding, and professionalism required to make their home purchase a rewarding and fulfilling experience.

❍ ❍ ❍ ❍

SECRET 7

Decoding Parking Solutions in Real Estate

Parking is an essential aspect to consider when buying a home, and understanding the details surrounding parking arrangements can significantly impact your overall living experience.

In this chapter, we delve into the nuances of parking provisions in real estate developments, focusing on stack parking solutions and their practicality in the context of Pune, India.

- **Inclusion of Parking in the Agreement:** It's vital to verify whether the parking space is clearly demarcated and documented in the agreement. This ensures clarity and prevents any disputes regarding parking allocation in the future.
- **Practicality of Stack Parkings in Pune:** Investigate the viability and effectiveness of stack parking systems in Pune by visiting locations where such systems are in place. Determine if stack parking has evolved into a convenient solution or if it has posed challenges, such as rendering the space akin to a loft.
- **Developer's Intent Behind Stack Parking:** Understand why the developer has opted for stack parking facilities. Consider factors such as space optimization and maximizing parking capacity. Additionally, inquire about contingency plans in case of power outages, maintenance requirements, associated costs

for Annual Maintenance Contracts (AMC), and who bears the expenses for AMC.

- **Maintenance and Repair Concerns:** Evaluate the turnaround time for repairs on stack parking systems. Determine the implications for residents if the system malfunctions and the vehicle gets stuck. Find out the frequency of breakdowns and the measures in place to minimize disruptions to residents.

By investigating these aspects of parking solutions, particularly stack parking arrangements, you can make informed decisions regarding their convenience, reliability, and long-term satisfaction with their chosen living space.

SECRET 8

Assessing Project Ageing and Maintenance

When purchasing a home, it's important to consider not just the immediate appeal and functionality, but also how well the project will age and what maintenance responsibilities you can expect. Understanding these factors can save you from unexpected costs and ensure your investment remains valuable and comfortable for years to come.

a. **Is This Project Designed to Age Slower?**

- **Exterior Paint and Cladding:** The quality of materials used on the exterior can significantly affect the longevity of the building. Investigate how many coats of paint have been applied to the exterior. More coats typically mean better protection against weathering. Additionally, check if stone cladding has been used in the main entrance areas for added durability and aesthetic appeal.
- **Ease of Cleaning:** Consider how easy it will be to clean the building premises. Materials that resist dirt and grime can reduce maintenance efforts and costs. One should check whether there are any parts of the structure that can't be accessed for cleaning.. such areas over time become ugly spots

- **Ageing of Equipment:** The longevity and efficiency of electronic equipment in a residential project play a significant role in maintenance costs and the overall living experience. Knowing the average age and expected lifespan of these components such as lifts (elevators), STPs (sewage treatment plans), and CC TVs can help you gauge future maintenance needs and potential replacements. Any signs of wear and tear, such as frequent breakdowns or slow performance, indicate the need for significant repairs or replacement.

b. **Handover Details**

- **Warranties & AMC:** Check whether the developer will hand over the warranties and annual maintenance contracts (AMCs) with the OEMs (original equipment manufacturers). Ensure that there is provision for the handover of all the electronic equipment that comes with warranties and AMCs to cover regular servicing and unexpected repairs.
- **Handover & Estate Management:** Is there a possession and handover manual in place to guide the Society to make informed decisions on maintenance post-handover? Also, find out what is the handover procedure. Will there be an Estate Manager or a single point of contact post-handover?

c. **Expected Maintenance Costs**

- **Corpus Fund:** Another area to check is whether the project has a big enough Corpus Fund.

One critical factor in the long-term maintenance and sustainability of a real estate project is the existence of a substantial corpus fund. A corpus fund is a large sum of money collected upfront from the homeowners, intended to cover future maintenance expenses and unforeseen costs.

Here's why a well-funded corpus is vital:

- **Subsidizing Monthly Maintenance Charges:** The interest earned from the corpus fund can significantly subsidize monthly maintenance charges, reducing the financial burden on residents.
- **Covering Periodic Maintenance Expenditures:** Regular painting of the exterior and interior common areas is essential to maintain the aesthetic appeal and protect the building from weather damage. A strong corpus fund ensures that these expenses are covered without needing additional contributions from residents.
- **Choosing to go Solar:** Investing in solar panels can reduce energy costs and promote sustainability. A robust corpus fund can support these initial investments and their periodic maintenance, making green energy accessible without extra charges.
- **Investing in Safety Netting:** Safety netting for balconies and windows, especially in high-rise buildings, ensures the safety of residents, particularly children and pets. The corpus fund can cover these installations and their upkeep, ensuring ongoing safety without additional costs.

A well-managed corpus fund represents financial foresight, planning for future expenses, and ensuring the project remains financially stable over the long term.

SECRET 9

Does The Project Have Monetization Opportunities?

A well-managed residential society can explore various monetization opportunities to generate additional revenue, which can help offset maintenance charges and enhance the community's financial health. Choosing such a project can help lessen the burden of maintenance costs on you.

Here are some key strategies to consider:

a. Renting Out Spaces for Private Functions

- **Community Halls and Common Areas:** If the society has a community hall, clubhouse, or other common areas, these can be rented out to residents for private functions such as parties, meetings, or celebrations. This provides a cost-effective venue for residents while generating additional income for the Society. Renting these spaces within the society premises offers convenience and often lower costs compared to external venues, making it an attractive option for residents.

b. Other Monetization Opportunities

- **Advertising Space:** Utilizing common areas such as notice boards, lobbies, and elevators for advertisements is a great monetization opportunity. Local businesses and service providers may be willing to pay for advertising space within the society premises. Additionally, installing digital displays in high-traffic areas can attract more advertisers and generate consistent revenue.

- **Parking Spaces:** Another monetization avenue is renting out unused parking spaces to residents or even non-residents if allowed. This can be especially lucrative in areas with limited parking availability. Implementing a nominal fee for guest parking can also contribute to the society's revenue.
- **Solar Energy:** Installing rooftop solar panels can not only reduce the Society's electricity expenses but also the excess energy can be adjusted with the grid for credits bringing down your bills.

All this information can help you choose a project that eases your burden of maintenance costs.

❍ ❍ ❍ ❍

SECRET 10

Know Your Neighbours and Community

When moving into a new home, the community and neighbors play a significant role in your overall living experience. Understanding who your neighbors are and whether the developer has taken steps to ensure a harmonious community is crucial.

Here's what you need to know and should check with your builder:

a. Disclosure of Neighbors

- Check if the developer is willing to disclose the names of the people living on your floor or in your building. This transparency helps you understand who you will be living alongside and can ease any concerns about unfamiliar faces.

b. Like-Minded Community

- Understanding the background of your neighbors is important to ensure a cohesive living environment. Are they professionals, families, or retirees? Knowing this can help gauge if the community aligns with your lifestyle and values. Check how is the layout of the project in terms of units, bottom line is that the expectations and lifestyles of a person investing in a 50 L unit and another in a 2.5 Cr unit may not match. Keep these practicalities in mind when deciding.

c. **Screening Process**

- Ask if the developer has a screening process for potential buyers. This ensures that the community is curated thoughtfully, preventing any disruptive or incompatible elements from moving in simply because they have the financial means.
- Developers with a vision for building a cohesive gated community of like-minded people tend to foster a more peaceful and cooperative living environment. Ask about the developer's intention and efforts in creating such a community.

Checking these points carefully will ensure that you not only zero down on your dream home but also have the privilege of being part of a positive, like-minded community.

SECRET 11

The Heartbeat of Development

Behind every towering structure and sprawling development lies the silent, yet profound, heartbeat of the labor force. Does your developer, understand and value this heartbeat? Is compassionate construction a core value & philosophy for your builder/developer?

Would you want to live in a home where the people who lay the very foundations of your dreams are not treated humanely and fairly?

a. Civic & Sanitation Needs

- Check how sensitive is the developer to the basic needs of the labor force? The answer lies in the genuine efforts made to ensure that the workforce feels valued and cared for.
- Are their camps/colonies in good civic conditions? Do they have access to potable water and clean toilets? Are they provided with basic medical facilities and aid at the very least?

b. Empowerment through Training

- Are they trained periodically? Training isn't a one-off event but a continuous journey of growth and empowerment. Esteemed institutes like Kushal, QCI, and NSDC can be invited to the site, providing on-site training that not only enhances skills but also boosts confidence and self-worth. Is the builder into such initiatives?

c. **Safety: A Sacred Commitment**

- Find out whether due labor safety measures are taken or not. Safety is sacred. Chose a builder who implements rigorous safety protocols ensuring that every worker operates in a secure environment. From protective gear to emergency drills, every measure should be taken to protect the laborers who build your future. Does the Developer have a safety officer? Are there periodic Safety Audits?

Secret 11 is more than just a set of practices; it's a reflection of who your builder truly is. You can be sure that a person/company that takes good care of its grassroots-level employees is bound to deliver great quality to its customers.

SECRET 12

Creating a Safe Haven for Your Children

As parents, your primary concern is the safety and well-being of your children and family. Moving into a new home is a monumental decision, and ensuring that your loved ones are protected is paramount.

Secret 12 is all about understanding the essential safety measures and features that should be in place to create a secure and nurturing environment for your children.

Here's what you should know about:

a. **Fire Safety: A Lifeline in Emergencies**

- **Fire safety is non-negotiable.** How often are fire drills conducted? Regular fire drills are crucial in ensuring that everyone knows how to respond to an emergency. Are the staircase and lift doors fire-rated? If so, for how many hours? These are critical questions. High fire ratings mean that these structures can withstand fire for a longer period, providing more time for safe evacuation.

b. **Theft and Privacy Measures: Peace of Mind**

- **When it comes to theft and privacy,** a minimum of 3-tier security is essential. This includes robust access control, vigilant security personnel, and advanced surveillance systems. Are there sufficient & efficient security personnel placed strategically? Are all entries manned & under surveillance with CCTV cameras covering major entry points? These cameras act as both a deterrent and a means to quickly respond to any suspicious activity, ensuring your family's privacy and safety.

c. **Proximity to Emergency Services: Vital Lifelines**

- **How close is the nearest police station or hospital?** In emergencies, time is of the essence. Quick access to these critical services can make a significant difference, offering reassurance that help is always nearby.

d. **Preventing Accidents: Safe Spaces for Kids**

- **Accidents,** such as children falling, can happen in an instant. What security measures are in place to prevent such incidents? Childproof locks, secure railings, and safety gates are just a few of the precautions that can create a safer environment for your little ones to explore and play.

e. **Technology for Enhanced Safety: Smart Solutions**

- Technology plays a pivotal role in modern safety measures. Apps like MyGate offer a seamless way to manage security, providing real-time updates and control over who enters the community. This technology empowers you with the tools to keep your family safe and secure.

f. **Lift and Equipment Safety: Reliable and Secure**

- Lift safety is critical. Are the lifts and other equipment from reliable manufacturers and are they regularly maintained and inspected? Regular maintenance ensures that these essential services operate smoothly and safely, preventing accidents and ensuring reliability.

Secret 12 is about creating a sanctuary where your children can thrive without you constantly worrying about their safety. It's about knowing that the necessary precautions are in place, giving you peace of mind and allowing your family to focus on what truly matters — creating cherished memories together.

As home-buyers, ensuring these safety measures are in place is not just a priority; it's a necessity. Your children's safety is your greatest responsibility, and by making informed choices, you can provide them with a safe, loving, and nurturing environment.

❍ ❍ ❍ ❍

SECRET 13

The Green Haven The Role of Landscaping in Home-buying

When envisioning your dream home, the landscape plays a crucial role. It's not just about aesthetics; it's about creating a green haven that enhances your quality of life. Understanding the details of the landscape design can reveal how much thought and care has been put into creating a space that you and your family will love.

Here's what to check on:

a. Tree Selection: A Breath of Fresh Air

- What kind of trees should you expect? The types of trees selected for a property can significantly impact its ambience and air quality. The landscape should have trees that provide shade, beauty, and oxygen are ideal. Also, check if the trees chosen are native and adaptive species for their resilience and environmental benefits.
- Is the consultant known for their tree selection? A reputable landscape consultant is essential. They bring expertise in selecting the right trees that thrive in the local climate and soil conditions. Their knowledge ensures a lush, sustainable, and beautiful environment.

Also check for the Specific Tree Categories and their numbers being planted on the project.

1. **Fruit-Bearing Trees:**
    - These trees not only enhance the beauty of the landscape but also provide fresh produce. The consultant selects fruit trees that are well-suited to the local environment and can thrive with minimal maintenance.
2. **Fragrant Trees:**
    - Fragrant trees add a sensory dimension to the landscape, offering pleasant scents that enhance the outdoor experience.
    - The consultant can recommend a variety of fragrant trees such as magnolias, jasmine, or gardenias, ensuring they are strategically placed to maximize their aromatic benefits.
3. **Spiritual and Herbal Plants:**
    - These plants can hold cultural or spiritual significance and also offer medicinal benefits.
    - The consultant can include trees and plants such as tulsi (holy basil), neem, sandalwood, and others known for their spiritual and herbal properties.

By leveraging the expertise of a reputable landscape consultant, property owners can create a lush, sustainable, and beautiful environment that meets their aesthetic, functional, and cultural needs. The consultant's detailed knowledge of tree selection ensures that every aspect of the landscape, from fruit-bearing trees to fragrant and spiritual plants, contributes to a harmonious and thriving outdoor space.

b. Track Record of Excellence

- Check what other projects the landscape consultant delivered in the last five years. A consultant's portfolio reflects their capability and vision. Reviewing their past projects can give you insight into their design style, creativity, and attention to detail. It's reassuring to see successful, well-received projects they have completed.

c. Vision for Oxygen Infusion

- Does the landscape designer have a vision for oxygen infusion through trees? A thoughtful designer prioritizes planting trees that not only beautify the space but also enhance air quality. Trees known for their high oxygen production and air purification capabilities contribute to a healthier living environment.

d. Professional Design for Kids' Spaces

Is there a professional, detailed design in place for these places where kids will spend the majority of their time, or is it being developed without deep study and understanding of the end user? Spaces for children require special consideration. A well-designed playground, garden, or park can offer safety, engagement, and developmental benefits. Ensure that these areas are designed with a thorough understanding of children's needs, providing a safe and stimulating environment.

Secret 13 is about recognizing the importance of detailed and thoughtful landscaping in creating a holistic living experience. It's about ensuring that the green spaces around your home are not only beautiful but also functional, sustainable, and nurturing. A well-designed landscape reflects a commitment to enhancing your family's quality of life, offering spaces where you can relax, breathe, and enjoy nature's bounty. When buying a home, delving into the details of the landscape design can reveal much about the overall care and consideration invested in the property.

❍ ❍ ❍ ❍

SECRET 14

End-Use Design Ethos/Philosophy for Your Dream Home

When choosing a home, it's essential to consider how well it suits your daily routines and lifestyle. Thoughtful design is not just about aesthetics; it's about ensuring every aspect of your home is tailored to meet the needs of its residents. Secret 14 delves into the end-use design philosophies that transform a house into a truly comfortable and functional home.

Here's what you should enquire about:

a. Routine Considerations in Design

- What are some end-use studies done by the developer? Developers who conduct end-use studies understand how future residents will live in their homes. These studies inform design choices that enhance comfort and convenience.
- Has the developer studied the morning, afternoon, and evening routines of the end-user to design the apartment? For example, how many members will use the bathrooms between 5 am and 9 am? Designing with these routines in mind ensures that spaces like bathrooms and kitchens are optimized for peak usage times, preventing bottlenecks and enhancing comfort.

b. Privacy and Practicality

- Has the architect taken privacy into account when designing for guests, outsiders, and the domestic staff? Ensuring privacy from guests and service areas is crucial for creating a sense of sanctuary. Thoughtful layouts that separate public and private spaces contribute to a more harmonious living environment.

c. Convenience in Layout

- Check whether the architect has designed the homes in a manner that incorporates ease of movement and small conveniences such as a wash basin next to the dining area so one doesn't need to enter a wet bathroom or kitchen after eating. Simple conveniences like this enhance daily living and maintain hygiene standards.

d. Luxury Features

- Walk-in wardrobes and balconies to the master bedroom etc. are features that add luxury and practicality. Walk-in wardrobes offer ample storage and organization, while balconies provide private outdoor space for relaxation. Make sure that these are a part of the architecture of your unit.

e. Maximizing Views and Ventilation

- Check whether the project offers ample ventilation along with aesthetics. Wall-to-wall windows ensure maximum views of the vibrant skyline. These windows not only provide stunning views but also allow natural light to flood the home, creating a bright and inviting atmosphere. However, there has to be a balance between vows, ventilation & heat control. Heat, light, and ventilation studies, including sun-path and wind-path analyses, ensure windows are designed to optimize ventilation and light while reducing heat. These considerations lead to a more energy-efficient and comfortable home.

f. **Functional Utility Spaces**

- Separate dry balconies & utility areas ensure the house does not smell like detergent, providing a designated area for laundry, cleaning supplies, broom, mops etc. Additionally, clothes-drying equipment as an amenity further enhances this functionality.

g. **A Balanced Design Philosophy**

- A design philosophy that distinguishes between glamorous and non-glamorous places ensures each space serves its intended purpose while maintaining overall harmony. Public spaces like living rooms and kitchens should be both functional and stylish, while private spaces prioritize comfort and privacy.
- The design of public and private spaces within the home should reflect their distinct uses. Public areas should be welcoming and social, while private areas should offer solitude and relaxation.

Secret 14 is about appreciating the intricate details that go into designing a home that truly caters to your needs. By understanding your daily routines, prioritizing privacy, incorporating luxury features, and optimizing light and ventilation, developers and architects create spaces that are not only beautiful but also highly functional. When buying a home, look for these thoughtful design elements that ensure your living experience is as comfortable and enjoyable as possible.

SECRET 15

Mindfully Designed Amenities

How mindful was the design of amenities? Thoughtful amenities are not just about ticking boxes; they are about enhancing the quality of life for all residents. A well-planned community offers amenities that cater to diverse needs and are seamlessly integrated into the lifestyle of its inhabitants.

Here's what to consider:

a. Practicality and Usability

- Don't just be dazzled by the amenities on offer. Check whether the amenities will actually be used. Practicality is key. Amenities should be designed and located in a way that encourages regular use. This means considering the daily routines and preferences of residents to ensure the facilities are both convenient and inviting. Amenities also need to be Inclusive for all ages
- Check what amenities are there for senior citizens, toddlers, and teens. A well-rounded community provides spaces for all age groups. For senior citizens, this might include peaceful gardens, walking paths, and social areas. Toddlers need safe, engaging play areas, while teens benefit from spaces like game rooms, sports facilities, and study lounges.

b. Fitness Amenities: Health and Wellness

Find out what fitness amenities are there. A modern community should be able to offer a variety of fitness options. This could include a well-equipped gym, swimming pool, yoga studio, and outdoor exercise areas.

Find out if the fitness amenities are designed by fitness experts. Is the equipment chosen with the consultation of experts? Fitness amenities should be developed with input from professionals to ensure they meet the needs of all users. Expert consultation ensures the right mix of equipment and facilities for effective and safe workouts.

- How big is the gym? Is it big enough for the number of residents? A well-sized gym ensures that all residents have ample space and equipment to exercise without overcrowding.
- What kind of flooring will the multi-purpose playground have? What kind of flooring will the jogging track have? Durable, safe, and comfortable flooring materials are crucial for outdoor activities. The playground should have soft, impact-absorbing surfaces, while the jogging track requires a resilient, non-slip surface to enhance the running experience.
- How big is the pool? Is it designed for hassle-free maintenance? The pool should be large enough to accommodate multiple users comfortably and designed with easy maintenance in mind to ensure it remains clean and inviting.
- Is the basketball court designed professionally, a professionally designed basketball court would feature

high-quality materials for the surface, providing excellent grip and durability to withstand regular use. Proper lighting is crucial for evening play, ensuring the court is well-illuminated without glare. Ensuring these elements are in place confirms that the basketball court is suitable for both casual and competitive play, enhancing the overall recreational value of the property.

c. **Entertainment Amenities: Longevity and Impact**

- Are the entertainment amenities designed for longevity and impactful use? Long-lasting and versatile entertainment amenities like home theaters, community halls, and recreational rooms enhance social life. These spaces should be durable, easy to maintain, and adaptable to various activities.
- Does the home-theater space have internet connectivity? Can there be a child lock on content in the home theater? Modern home theaters should be equipped with high-speed internet and parental controls to ensure a safe and enjoyable experience for all ages.
- Knowing whether the builder includes an indoor game area in the project is crucial, as these facilities can greatly enhance the quality of life for residents. Look for details on what facilities are available, such as table tennis, billiards, squash courts, and multipurpose rooms for activities like yoga or aerobics. Additionally, confirm the availability of comfortable seating areas and proper ventilation, which are important for maintaining a pleasant indoor environment. Checking these aspects ensures that the indoor amenities meet your expectations and contribute to a comfortable and enjoyable lifestyle.

- When evaluating a property, it's important to thoroughly check the renders and finishing of the indoor game areas. Ensuring that these spaces are well-designed and completed to high standards can significantly enhance the living experience. It's also essential to verify if the developer will be providing air conditioning in key indoor areas such as the gym and other recreational spaces.

d. Traffic Control: Safe and Efficient

- Ask about & understand how the traffic flow & control of the project is designed— how are the entry and exit points for vehicles and pedestrians placed, including designated pathways for pedestrians separate from vehicle routes— a well-designed traffic flow is essential for safety and efficiency. Properly designed traffic flow minimizes congestion and ensures the safety of all residents.

Secret 15 highlights the importance of thoughtfully designed amenities in creating a vibrant, functional, and inclusive community. By considering the needs of all age groups, ensuring practicality and expert input, and focusing on safety and usability, a well-planned community offers amenities that significantly enhance the residents' quality of life. When choosing a home, look for these carefully considered features that show a genuine commitment to resident satisfaction and well-being.

SECRET 16

The Art of Internal Layout

When it comes to creating a truly comfortable and functional home, the internal layout is a critical factor. It's more than just walls and rooms; it's about crafting a space that flows seamlessly and meets your unique needs. From ensuring privacy to optimizing natural light and ventilation, the internal design plays a significant role in your daily living experience. This secret will guide you through the essential elements to look for in an apartment layout, helping you find a home that balances practicality, privacy, and aesthetics perfectly.

Lookout for the following considerations:

a. Ensuring Privacy

- Can visitors of other apartments see inside your home from the entrance? How much can they see? Privacy is paramount in any home. The layout should ensure that neighbors or visitors cannot easily view the interior of your apartment from common areas.
- Can guests sitting in the living room see inside any bedrooms? It's essential to have a clear sepiaration between public and private spaces. Your living room should be designed to maintain privacy for the bedrooms, ensuring that your personal spaces remain undisturbed even when entertaining guests.

- Is there the possibility for you to install a door that can separate public and private spaces in your apartment? The ability to create a physical barrier between living areas and private quarters is crucial. This separation helps maintain privacy and reduces noise, enhancing comfort and tranquility within your home.

b. Entrance Foyer for Privacy and Noise Reduction

- Does the home have an entrance foyer? Verify the presence of a private alleyway or foyer space at the entrance. An entrance foyer acts as a buffer zone, providing a sense of separation from the outside world. It shields your home from direct visibility and noise, creating a welcoming and private entryway.

c. Balconies & Break-Out Spaces

- Check how many balconies does the apartment have. Are the balonies spacious? What is the view from the balconies?
- Master bedrooms in larger apartments must have a break-out space. Balconies provide a private outdoor area for relaxation, fresh air, and enjoying the view. They enhance the living experience by offering a seamless indoor-outdoor connection.

d. Walk-In Wardrobes for Ample Storage

- Checking for walk-in wardrobes is a must— with increasing personal possessions, at least one bedroom must have large walk-in wardrobes. Ample storage is essential for modern living. Walk-in wardrobes offer organized space for clothing and personal items, keeping your bedroom clutter-free and enhancing functionality.

e. **Optimizing Natural Light, Heat, and Ventilation**

- Consider the natural light, heat, and ventilation of the units. A well-designed layout maximizes natural light, providing a bright and welcoming atmosphere. Proper ventilation ensures fresh air flow, while thoughtful placement of windows and insulation helps regulate temperature, reducing the need for artificial heating and cooling.

f. **Standard-Sized Furniture in Layouts and Sample Flats**

- Check the size of the furniture placed in the layout or sample flat. Ensure it's standard size. The layout should accommodate standard-sized furniture comfortably, reflecting realistic living conditions. Oversized or undersized furniture can mislead buyers about the actual space available.

This secret emphasizes the importance of a well-thought-out internal layout in creating a comfortable and functional living space. From ensuring privacy and separation of spaces to optimizing natural light and ventilation, each aspect contributes to the overall quality of your home. When evaluating a potential home, pay close attention to these details, as they significantly impact your daily living experience and long-term satisfaction. Thoughtful design enhances not only the aesthetics but also the practicality and enjoyment of your living space.

❍ ❍ ❍ ❍

SECRET 17

The Heart of Your Home
The Kitchen

The kitchen is often considered the heart of the home, a place where meals are prepared, conversations flow, and memories are made. It's a space that should blend functionality with comfort and style, ensuring it meets the diverse needs of daily living and special occasions alike.

From its layout and size to the materials used and the natural light it receives, every aspect of the kitchen contributes to the overall harmony of your home.

This secret will delve into the key factors that make a kitchen not just a cooking space, but a cornerstone of household happiness and efficiency.

Here's what you need to consider:

a. Location

- Ensure that the kitchen is located close to the entry door, the living room, or the dining area, as per your preference. The kitchen's position should enhance the flow of your daily routines and make meal preparations more convenient. It should also be close to the utility area for easy operations.
- A kitchen near the dining area simplifies entertaining, while an accessible utility area keeps supplies handy.

Check their proximity for convenience. This arrangement makes serving meals more efficient and keeps everything you need within easy reach.

b. Size of the Kitchen

- Check if the kitchen is spacious and can accommodate all the essential appliances you need. The space should be adequate for daily as well as occasional needs. A well-sized kitchen makes cooking enjoyable and efficient, providing ample room for all your culinary adventures.

c. Type of the Kitchen — Open, Closed, or Semi-Open

- Evaluate the kitchen design and planning closely to ensure it aligns with your cooking style, need for interaction, privacy, comfort, and family preference. Whether you prefer an open layout that integrates with living spaces, a closed kitchen for privacy, or a semi-open design for the best of both worlds, make sure it suits your lifestyle.

d. Visibility to and from the Kitchen

- The kitchen's location should prioritize both access to outside views, through a door or window, as well as privacy. A kitchen with a pleasant view and good visibility enhances the cooking experience, while strategic placement ensures privacy from other areas of the home.

e. Influx of Natural Light and Ventilation

- Verify if the kitchen design allows ample natural light and good airflow to minimize odors and reduce electricity usage. A bright, well-ventilated kitchen is not only more pleasant to work in but also more energy-efficient and healthier.

f. **The Platform**

- **Dimension:** Ensure the kitchen platform fits your preferences and needs in shape, size, height, and depth, ensuring functional design. The right dimensions make cooking and cleaning more comfortable, preventing strain and enhancing workflow.
- **Material:** The platform material should be aesthetic, durable, easy to maintain and wash, and should be resistant to scratching and chipping. A high-quality platform material not only looks good but also stands up to daily wear and tear, making it a practical choice for the long term.
- **Platform Length:** Verify if the platform accommodates multiple people comfortably for cooking, with space for a hob/stove, daily use items, and standard cabinets.

g. **The Kitchen Triangle**

- Verify the hob/stove, refrigerator, and sink placement for efficiency, focusing on the kitchen triangle's functionality.

h. **The Sink**

- Check the sink convenience, nearby bin placement, drain space, hot water access, and tap suitability for your needs.

i. **Storage Space Available**

- Verify there is ample storage under and above the platform for daily items. Extra space is ideal for customizable storage solutions.

j. **Space for Kitchen Appliances and Electrical Points**

- Ensure the kitchen layout allows for convenient placement of appliances like the refrigerator, microwave, and dishwasher. Also, confirm ample and strategically placed electrical points for their usage.

h. Ease of Maintenance and Cleaning

- Confirm that the kitchen floor tiles, dado tiles, and platform surface are easy to clean, maintaining a tidy and hygienic space despite regular cooking activities.
- The importance of a well-designed kitchen in creating a harmonious and efficient home cannot be emphasized enough— From its location and size to the type and materials used, each aspect of the kitchen should be carefully considered to meet your needs and preferences.

A thoughtfully planned kitchen becomes the heart of the home, a place that not only feeds mouths & stomachs but nurtures relationships and strengthens family bonds are strengthened. When evaluating a potential home, ensure the kitchen is designed with care, providing a functional, comfortable, and aesthetically pleasing space for all your culinary endeavors.

❍ ❍ ❍ ❍

To Sum It All Up!

Congratulations on reaching the end of
"Zero Anxiety Home-Buying- 17 Must-Know Secrets Before Buying Your Dream"

By now, you have gained valuable insights and practical knowledge that will serve you well as you navigate the home-buying process. Armed with these secrets, you are now better prepared to make informed decisions, avoid common pitfalls, and ultimately find the home that best suits your needs and desires.

Throughout this book, we have covered a wide range of topics, each secret has been carefully chosen to address the most critical aspects of buying a home, ensuring that you have a comprehensive understanding of what it takes to succeed in this endeavor.

Remember, the journey to homeownership is unique for everyone. Your circumstances, priorities, and preferences will shape your experience. Use the knowledge you've gained from this book to tailor your approach, stay flexible, and remain patient. The perfect home for you is out there, and with the right strategies and mindset, you will find it.

As you move forward, keep these final thoughts in mind:

➢ **Stay Informed:** The real estate market is constantly evolving. Stay updated on market trends and continue educating yourself about the home-buying process.

- **Seek Professional Advice:** While this book provides a solid foundation, don't hesitate to seek advice from real estate professionals, financial advisors, and legal experts when needed.
- **Trust Your Instincts:** Buying a home is not just a financial decision; it's an emotional one too. Trust your instincts and ensure that the home you choose feels right for you and your family.
- **Be Patient:** Finding the right home may take time. Don't rush the process. Be patient and wait for the home that meets your criteria and feels the right fit.
- **Choose Your Builder/Project Carefully:** From The 17 secrets shared here, choose the ones that matter to you, prioritize all of them in your order of preference, list your non-negotiables, and then assess & benchmark the properties you are considering basis your list and voila you will zero in on your dream home!

Thank you for allowing me to be part of your home-buying journey. I hope the secrets shared in this book have empowered you and given you the confidence to make wise and informed decisions. May your new home bring you joy, comfort, and countless happy memories.

Also, I would be delighted to hear about your house-hunting experiences and the benefits you received as a result of using the 17 secrets presented in this book. In your experience which secrets proved to be the most valuable for you? Or did you encounter any obstacles in digging deep? Your feedback & your suggestions would be incredibly helpful and will have a big impact on my current work and upcoming publications.

Furthermore, don't hesitate to get in touch with me if you have any queries or want to learn more about these ideas.

You can write to me at-

nilesh@kanchandevelopers.com

Wishing you the very best in your home-buying adventure!

❍ ❍ ❍ ❍